READER PRAISE FOR *THE LIGHT BETWEEN US*

"[Beth] Morey gives us flawed but oh-so-real characters that linger long in memory. I found myself rooting for Ruth and Derek, delighted by their love story, foibles and all. [She] is a novelist to look out for."

"This book is a touching love story that reminds us that love knows no time, it has no boundaries and it *can* happen when you least expect it."

"I loved how this book jumped over societal norms to embrace love when it came."

" This is the first book I've read by Ms. Morey, but it will not be the last. *The Light Between Us* is such an enjoyable read that I look forward to reading it again; it has definitely made my re-read list."

"I couldn't stop reading it! I loved the story's flow and the artistry in how the author wrote."

"It is billed as a 'romance', which scared me, because my thoughts immediately went to Jilly Cooper or 50 Shades of overly-explicitness and badly-written dialogue, but I was relieved that it wasn't like that. In fact, die-hard romance fans might think there is too little sex in there, but I thought it was right: tastefully tantalising. Perhaps this is romance for non-romance-readers? I really enjoyed the characterisation, and particularly liked the fact that it was a love story where the heroine was both quietly introverted and feisty. Beth writes redemption and forgiveness really well, and I thoroughly enjoyed this light and well-written love story. It's cheap as an e-book, and would make excellent beach reading for the summer."

"I loved the honesty in the characters. I loved how they were flawed but still hopeful. The story was interesting and sweet, I didn't want to put it down."

"*The Light Between Us* kept me entertained and

engaged from beginning to end. The book was full of plot twists and yet it came complete with a feel good ending. Morey is a talented author, and I look forward to reading more of her books in the future!"

"We need more of [Morey] in the indie world."

ALSO BY BETH MOREY:

The Light Between Us

Life After Eating Disorder

NIGHT CYCLES

NIGHT CYCLES

poetry for a dark night of the soul

by Beth Morey

for Jacob and Eamon – may you always live the questions

CONTENTS

the spiritual disciplines

The Beetle

Yarrow

my words are a whisper, my words are a
howl

the night visitor

in the darkness

when I am missing you

lives

rustlings

our note of apology to the future

spoiled epiphanies (or, when the poet is
broken)

ASCENT

lineage

on the impossible

the letter

she remembers

rebirthing

He

egress

on the longest night

woman rising

swell

THE LIGHT (or something like it)

on rising

incarnation

reflections from a shop of recycled
          homewares

the gray hair

playing house

red

I am

a blessing for the living

cadence

the god I'll bow down to

song for the darkness

the wildest one

do you dare to step in-
to the vulnerable black, stripped
to the soul with human blindness –

when the full and weeping
moon steps from the shade
of a tumult of mountains –

when, in the fragrant dim,
day's tree stump transforms
into some nether-worldly other –

when time's skin is thin and you are
bared – when there is nothing
between you and the Wildest One

whose name is your own?

DESCENT

wrestling rusted doubt

wrestling rusted doubt
knowing is my idol
speak, your servant aches to listen
reach down your holy calloused palm

knowing is my idol
keep this body red and breathing
reach down your holy calloused palm
can we weep together?

keep this body red and breathing
speak, your servant aches to listen
can we weep together?
wrestling rusted doubt

love limping home
(a found poem)

I have lived so long in this land,
a knife of glass upon the heart.

no fear. I had a dream of the great
Mother in the hidden valley,
never found.

many lives ago
the war priests guarded the secret.
one showed me a map. I'm
going there now, boots already
ancient with your dust.

(your mind only knew
part of the story.
my heart told the rest.)

night kissing

it looked like night kissing
at first, her lips pressing hot
against his on the snowy corner
outside the bowling alley

but a trawl of light shows
it's really her head on his shoulder,
fingers pressing comfort
through downy winter coats

and I wonder what freezes
the flurry of hurt on her cold-
flushed cheeks, if his touch is
a salve or the shattering

you say

you say
we were never
meant for this vowed life,
golden bands of only us, and death
do us part. you
say love like it's held in quotation marks,
that this union soured before
it started. no passion, no throbbing desire floods
your veins when you look
at me. all your slated glimpse can spy
is graying hairs and promises dulled
by your wavering. i can't make you hard-
falling for me, for this pact
we sealed with the birth-blood
of our son. You say you'd be gone
if not for him, only two years of breath
and his heart is already scarred
by our tepid affections. you say
you'd like some adventure, and I suspect
"adventure" looks like a blonde in cut-offs,
tanned flesh a decade younger than the bed
we share in silence. you say you think
you will follow your heart after all, after

her, and I say:

what of when her humanity bleeds
too thick through her skin, when you wake
in the morning to a mortal wearing old
mascara and folds around her eyes?
when she asks you to hold her soiled
soul as softly as she's held yours, or
to empty the overflowing trash (these are two
whispers of the same song), or to be here, be
here, be hers, like you said, you said,
you said you would. what of when she still
loves you after all the callous complaints
she's choked on in the name of your catharsis?
what of when she cries as she watches
your flame flutter and die, when all she wants
is for your breath to waft her way once
more?

you say, that will never be, moving
toward the door. I say, it already
is.

in between

she slips along
the sidewalk with a belly full
of baby [again] and only poetry
books tucked up
in her arm's crook and
she prays to feel as powerful
as she might if God sang silent
words into her ear and answered
all the rattling questions
      now

rainbow

his ribs carve delicate
about his flickering heart and
rise, fall against
my own, deep and
profound as a whale's dive,
regular as a clock. I won't
mark time with these
breaths, the shivery
waiting for an end hammering
a(nother) chink where
the fear slips in. kissing
into his soft halo of golden strands,
smelling the sweet-sour human
smell, my soul slips
off its sandals at
                  all this holy.

                          it seems impossible
                              that we never
                                    had this
                                    with her.

old ways
(a found poem)

suppose the secret died
with the last guardian, the ancient
who stood at the gate in the valley
and saw the sacred
vein of gold.

God,
is there no faith left?
He has not told. I
would not know Him if I saw Him.

holy saints defend
the truth, trembling.

on the dying of David's child

the old king clawed fetid, faithful heat
from his hollows and kissed the salt-
edge of his sword to skin and prayed
for rain in the desert of sickness and grief.

he gathered his graying tear-tangled beard
in weakening fists and wrenched the follicles
from their beds, a ravaged plot. he beat
his weathered form to the floor to buoy

his ragged prayers toward Holy.
he collected his queen and her women
in the bleeding chamber to wail with him
like wild cats of the anointed hill country

but the rattle shook silent in the child's
throat and the supplications of the old
king shattered in the air, slashing
his soul to pieces in their falling.

disintegration

white daisies on the grave
it's my fingers that drop
them there (did they?
i can't recall)
i am a vapor of sorrow

petals -- no, tears
that don't exist
ease down cheeks
i used to have, falling
on earth's dust, phantom

lungs throb with breath
i choke on the ash of sadness
i would keen if i could, if
i was anything
more than wilted legs and

these two hands
empty of daisies dolled
up in white death. i
think i died, too, the day
the sky hung like a portent,

mortar-heavy with meaning

iconography

the people gather and cling
to profane deity too smooth
and ceramic to root the heart
into, a shallow, fallow porcelain
ground. it is an anathema
of numbness, monotonous and safe
in its monotony.

the souls have never felt
such fetid and unaffected fervor.

Pathways to God

I thought it was supposed to be straight and
narrow, this way. That's what everyone said, after
all. *He* said it, too.

So I tried to live straight, tried to walk that narrow
line. I clenched my jaw and my buttocks and
pushed away all questions and the not-knowing
that threatened to cross my tightrope path.

They told me to walk this way, and keep walking.
But when I looked down and saw that the way that
I had been following had cut off like the end of a
movie reel, film flapping freely as it circles and
circles and circles, they didn't have much to say.

Not much that was new, anyway.

What now, I pleaded. My narrow way has left off,
and the world is howling wild around me. Can't you
see my bleeding places?

No, they said. You are not bleeding at all. Keep
walking, keep walking our way.

I tried. I tried. (I think. I hope.) I am tired. And the sure thing that everyone else seems to see is nowhere to be found for me.

I am blind in the dark place.

What now? What now?

I close my eyes, because what does it matter when vision has failed me? I slide a foot forward along the glassy ground that I've been treading, certain that I will feel all that is solid fall away beneath my toes, that I will leave my breath behind as I plummet down and down and through and into the vacuum of the lost.

I am at the gates of my own destruction.

(Or so I'm told.)

But instead of the cliff edge and the gaping, noiseless howl, my sole meets earth, rough and gritty. One more trembling foot forward, and then another, and soon I learn to breathe again. Or perhaps I take my first true breath, and anyway, it is not the poison I thought it would be.

I hear talk of that slippery slope, and my heart catches for a beat. But there is the musky truth I'm standing in that I can't deny, and it tastes of so much holy. That old way, the narrow line, I see now that was a slippery, saccharine surface where my soul could gain no purchase. For the first time, my feet feel sure beneath me, and that sense is twining its way up from my ankles, racing toward my knees, my thighs, my secret places, my heart. It's in my blood now, and I can't deny it. I can't deny it.

I open my eyes, because I could see even through my clutched-closed lids that the darkness is light, that the blindness has given way to searing vision.

I can't deny it.

THE DARK

the spiritual disciplines

we have forgotten what night tastes like,
salted by full moon silver rupturing
the dark. we have forgotten how the skin
sings when the lunar fervor unfurls
across its follicles.

we have forgotten that we were born
of celestial cataclysm.

we have forgotten how to dance
bare-footed on the earth to the cadence
of our souls. we have forgotten the ritual
fires and the acrid tang of holy smoke
on our tongues.

we have forgotten how to breathe.

we have forgotten how our voices
could resonate from the gut, strong,
together. we have forgotten that we are
made for birthing love.

we have forgotten how to press our fingers

to the tilting planet's jugular and measure
her pulse. we have forgotten symbiosis,
that she is our mother.

we have forgotten that when we rape
our world we rape ourselves.

we have forgotten that we belong
to each other, twined by breath and bone.
we have forgotten that our neighbors'
names are *me*, that *us* and *them* is
really *we*.

we have forgotten.
we have –

The Beetle

She did not see him there,
the beetle on her stoop. Bounding
down, the girl crushed him
unawares, and on her trip back
up the stairs she saw
the broken body

and she stopped
and sat,
watching his limbs tremble
in the leaving, reaching
helplessly for the hem
of life's skirt as it sashays away.

She aches to comfort him but
does not know the vigil clicks
of beetle-speak to companion him
in his dying. So she only leans
her face close, breathing
as his spark falters
into darkness, and she trembles
with her own knowing
that one day, in not too long

a time, it will be her crumpled
form twitching into eternity
on some shadowed concrete.

She grinds her sole
against the beetle to end
the suffering she began, death
creeping in on a summer day.

Yarrow

Yarrow is what she whispers
as we lay our head down to night
with its dream diving. "Are you
sure?" I mumble, lips pressing
pillowcase. *Yes*, she's certain, and too
sassy for these tiny hours, but she
prods, I groan and roll, scribble
the name on some scrap so she'll sanction
slumber. I extinguish the light and
darkness bleeds back in and my soul un-furls
      (her name is Yarrow) –   Sunrise and
searching, the internet speaks
of legend and devils, witch's nettle
and second sight and I wonder
what she's gotten us into, oh my
soul, my soul and I. S*acred herbs, divining
druids*, she thrills as I read and I can't
help my heart from throbbing
heavy, our blood leaping as if coming
home to one we haven't yet known.
      *Women of knowing, plantain poultices,
healing teas, visions of longing – I can
go on*, she teases.

"Please," I sigh and I won't
add "don't" this time. From our insides
she kisses these lips, breasts, fingertips.

I see and begin to see that I am
(we are) the arrow's root, a snake slinking in
the grass, an ancient seal. I can't
deny, our skin spreads already brighter,
leaf-lighter, air and ash a smudgy circlet
of freedom.

my words are a whisper, my words are a howl

I bowed down at the altar of *should* and *ought to* and *don't trust that dissembling soul of yours*. I pressed my forehead hard against the prayer rug until the carpet fibers imprinted the skin there into the permanent creases born of a disembodied life lived for everyone else.

And then one day I feel something, silver-new and dissonant. It takes time, years, until I can name it for what it is – the hot-cold edge of a blade balanced on the back of my neck, ready to sever this half-life should I dare to shift against its pressures.

Perhaps you know the feeling, the ever leeching shallow wound of threat and exterior expectation, the sick and steely sharpness of good intentions against the tender flesh. Through these seemingly slight sufferings the soul can drain away and away and away.

The blade that was intended to keep me small, tame, safe – in the end it was, ironically, the blade itself that lit the fuse, unlocked the gate, cracked open this secretly fertile seed of a heart.

Slowly,

s l o w l y,

my temperature rose and my pulse turned fierce and I began to press up against the knife-edge, the fear, the shoulds, all the ways I lived dead. And yes, the blade at my neck began to slice deeper, dragging against bone at last, and yes, it hurt. And just when I feared that I had killed my self, that my rebel rising truly was all the selfish, oversensitive silliness that I'd been told it was –

my soul expanded within my being like the birthing of the universe, and hardly without knowing what I did, and yet Knowing it deeply, my leg kicked out, kicked that blade away, and

I stood tall

for the first time in an age or ever, blood from what was now my freedom wound flowing down my back, tangling in my hair, leaving crimson paths across my face from where the wind whipped my tendrils wild against my forehead, my cheeks, about my ember eyes.

I stand in my own power now, the questions of permission that I used to choke on for my every meal now dead in a fallen heap, and when they tell me that I will fall, I nod. *I will fall*, I reply, and

my words are a whisper
my words are a howl

I will fall , I say, *and the tumbling will be all my own*. The skinned palms and oozing knees are holy wounds, stigmata of my She.

I will catch my own spilled blood, and not a drop will be wasted.

the night visitor

Time sits on my chest, thick
and heavy, leans
forward and smacks
lips fat with assurance, his
sour aspirations humid
heat against my ear and
I shudder, stomach seething,
roiling with sick and where
is sleep and there, the fear
clamors over his tongue, out
with the spittle of his speaking
and stalks my tired soul, neurons
firing and devouring the syllables and
"hurry, hurry, my lover, there
is not, not ever time
enough and you are dying
every turning day," and he's
right, I can't deny it, but

I heave and rise in the night,
send his truant bulk tumbling into
the ether and he wasn't all
that heavy after all. I wipe

his breath from the curves
of my ear, my heart, and my
hands are cold but my fists are
hot on their insides, and yes,
the hours, the hours can't be
stopped but the races they run
won't stop my own
journey over sea and stone and
earth bloodied with wasted
history, and I refuse to be
another who bleeds her life
pulse into the abyss. I grit
my jaw, throw a soul-hand high
and catch hold of the banner
of bravery that is always,
always throbbing near for
those whose fingertips reach and

rise, and I sigh as mine close on
this pen, breath of restoration and
relief and "can I?" the fear begins but
I push that away, sending
it fleeing along the wretched
wake of Time the liar and I
do.

in the darkness

we've forgotten how to look
at each other, depths of soul and
sanctuary. we've abandoned the fine
art of clumsy tumult between
the sheets.

does my heart empty and fill
and empty to our love's acrid cadence?
do my veins and these telescoping
lungs throb for you, for
us?

these questions are far too hard
for the night, more devoid
of hope's satisfaction than
your arms are
of me.

when I am missing you

absence
looks like a lake bed flooded with sky
sounds like cotton howling
tastes like tear-stained pillows
smells like churning bile and burnt hair
feels like screaming agony, my heart dying and
dying

lives

time and memory telescope
and all the past spills
into unfathomable middle
distance, where i cannot
tell if it is a thought
or a day in the sun
that passes in that moment
our bodies spread,
still, across the sheets. i

cannot see if we are
infants or ancients, i
cannot tell one lifetime
from another, or see
where death draws
her inscrutable line between
what was and what is.

the mind is a treasure
trove, an almanac, a tomb.

rustlings

the trees stand
silent before our opulent
transgressions, but
this does not mean
we are innocent. they are

wiser than we.
they know their roots
are deeper than ours,
their survival surer
than ours, that we are
sounding only the toll
of our own destruction.

eternity approaches.
they taste it in the soil
we've ruined for ourselves.

they can be patient.

our note of apology to the future

      we had time. we didn't
know, refused to know it, eyes
and hearts turning blind from the vicious
work of these hands, raping
the forests, gagging the wolves' wild
howl, flooding the seas with the refuse
of our lust.

      and there were voices
crying out in the wilderness,
the gnashing of teeth and rending
of sackcloth garments as they let
themselves feel their souls
bleeding. but we wouldn't
listen.

      the beasts have known
our ruinous errors far longer
than we – the ocean turtles
who learned to live choking
on ash and plastic, the urban
fox with only gutters
to nestle her kits into, the calf raised

from filthy birth to trembling,
murderous death on poison and
claustrophobia, no mother's
milk or sweet grass or open sky to
soothe her.

        we wondered why,
as the earth turned hot, but our
complaints only found answers in air
conditioners. we

        could have changed
our heading, sailed for more
moderate waters. but we clutched
our comforts and religious fire
escape cards close, and now the earth
has

        risen against you.
now you are dying, our children, our
children! death does not end
our weeping.

spoiled epiphanies (or, when the poet is broken)

I sit here in the dark
night of my own raw
  soul and
pretend that I know what I am doing
  here, dragging
  ink across the skin
  of fallen trees, as if
the questions I bleed
have answers.

what is poetry if not seeing
  and feeling,
  and feeling, feelings
  running deep
and okay – do I see, notice
  the gray pigeon feathers that heave
  by on drafts of passing
  cars reeking, leaking gasoline fumes
and okay – do I feel?

  oh, I've felt it all, the feeling
it lays thick

over this heart like
a callous that is not protecting,
  not healing, not
  a callous
  at all.
death and birth and
all that falls in the fleeting gasp of breath, oh
  I have known you
  too well
  too well.

what
does this pen run
with if not the amniotic rush
of learning all this hushed
  and holy heart-breaking-open
and standing witness
  to my own golden, squalid, spoiled
  incense-scented epiphanies?

I sit here, in the dim
iron excavation of the soul (it heals,
  I'm told) and
trust that I am – we
are all – I am

I am
doing the best I can.

ASCENT

lineage

imagine the desert
mothers, with hair tangled
tighter than their theology
and breasts that flowed milk
and mystic wisdom. they
knew how to draw the singing
sigils in the sand, how to dig
rough and bitten fingers
into desiccated dirt for water
to wet the lips of their young.

women of hips and heft, who
learned how to burn
beneath the wild and searing
sun, who made loud love
against the star-flecked threat
of night, who knew that strength
is not always a matter of muscle.

imagine your ancestresses,
the prophetesses of the arid
lands, before these starched
traditions and pews too hard

to pray from, who bled true
ritual and birthed their own fierce
souls at creation's crowning --

      stand at this door and, knock-
      ing, wonder what our sterile
      fall has wrought, what
      this moral rot has bought
      our gathering children.

on the impossible

the strength meets
me where I've forgotten
to expect it –

a fire needs
only the smallest spark
to ignite in
        surprise –

the letter

the little boy walks and does not bend
at the knees. he stumbles, sometimes,
sometimes sports the swollen lip
to prove it, but the sting won't stop

him, unlike his mother. she shushes
her soul to silence, bleeds and bleeds
at having listened to the world lisping
at her to play safe, breathe shallow,

and she listened, oh god, she listened
but she loves him, tells him anyway:

> *hold tight to your brave,*
> *child, clutch it close and let*
> *its rhythms flex the fingers and lead*
> *the feet to stepping, striding,*
> *falling, falling open. your soul is*
> *made for dancing, embroidered*
> *by energy, stitched with light.*
> *you were born for belly laughter*
> *and heaving sobs, nothing*
> *lukewarm about these sticky,*

steaming hearts of ours.
you were not born to live halfway.
fight for the deepening.

she wonders for the first time,
the thought a marvel, if she could, too.

she remembers

she forgets everyday, almost,
usually, just about – but today
she remembers

today, today, she remembers and
her spine grows long and deep, soul
cord winding umbilical down through the ages
of silt and soil, rainbow striations of salt
and ancient petrified bodies, down
to the roiling core, down to fire and flame,
down to impossible heat at the center

of all things. she roots to the Mother
and volcanic crimson pulses up and in
and she can breathe easy again, at last.
she remembers her true name. she

remembers the deep knowing, the sacred
howl, the dripping breasts and holy blood,
the wandering moon, the lion inside,
the ecstatic altar of love-making,
the bared feet meeting the night-black
earth in the wild dance. she remembers

the pride and the wolf pack, and how she is
a creature of cycles and claws, of rhythm
and abandon and untamed curls.

she fills with the fire, and it lances
her loneliness and the learned lies that haunted
her growing and her wilting. she remembers,
and her petals recolor, her putrid desiccation
falls away when, today, she remembers
who she is.

rebirthing

her soul groans
at her birthing,
the birth of her
own self,
the She she always
and never was

emerges at the
last, crowning,
and the soul
cries and writhes
and does not
know why her
muscles labor
and bind, clench
and petal open,
spirit labia
stretching,
thinning, tearing,
sighing at the
rising of her
own new
life.

her arms catch
the screaming
pink squall
anointed in blood,
curls her
babe-self close
and feeds her(self)
at the breast,
lets herself
down into her
self, the hungry
suckling her
rebirthed ears'
first capture.

She is safe.
She is wild.
She is here,
now,
at last.

He
(a found poem)

He will answer, eyes
bright. shining,
he rose and
approached his daughters in
a tongue the others did not understand,
words never meant
for them.

He beckoned, turned towards her
a face old,
old, mercy on love carrying
her away.

He said, clear, "I come
from the north, I come
to you from the truth, I
of the Sacred Three."

egress

words of this cracking
feel overdone, the bird
birth of my heart opening to
a catastrophe of breath and light
clumsy on the tongue –

but
i feel the spring breeze ruffling
the new-hatched damp of my unfurling
feathers; i see with eyes bleary from egg-dark
the shell clinging sticky to my screaming
beak; i feel the gasping comfort of my mother's
warm bulk, the food she chews and swallows for
me,
the nest she's built of twigs and tendriling vines,
a bit of turquoise thread –

and i know
my soul was never
more herself than this moment –
yolk proven and yielding skin and sinew and
a body formed for flying

on the longest night

solstice. I catch moon
crystals in my curls and dust
through snow of confetti sparkle.
clouds press close, and
feel safe. the velvet vault
of night is dark, but
rich and deep, our
eternal solitude, the soul-
growing expanse of eons
mapped by the muddy pulse
of the heart. we forget
we are not alone
in the lonely, the long
slumber, the blind seeing.

woman rising

three decades flipped by like nothing, like
a motion picture book, pages breathing
across the child's faces as she bends in close,
and all these days I've kept my eyes down
on the cold brick flood that never, never
warms, promising myself that this was good,
born from holy bone and righteous dust. but

now I'm blinking in a new gloaming
and all I see as I'm stretched low down here
is a world of women flat on their frozen
faces. we are the ground itself, corporeal
carpet of cells, softness calloused hard
beneath the pebbled soles of the fathers
and husbands and brothers and priests

and it's a horror if you could see it,
a world of women ruined
by man's fear. but here and there

the feminine surges, a woman on her knees
now, on her feet, rising, running, fire-
breathing. she may meet a fist with her teeth,

enamel shattering down our chins, but we
keep breaching like so many whales,
struggling to stand as tall as we're made.

And – we're making it, wild
haired, eyes hatching hope,
hearts kindling the key
for every locked and gnarled chain.
our collective cosmic She recalls
how alive the wakened woman is
and roars for the return
of her power in bleeding
and birthing and offering breast,
remembers the lioness tribe,
remembers remembers remembers.

the wick is lit and living, and so are We.
a world of women rising.

swell

we were taught to be small, live small, talk small,
love small, think small.

the ones who promised they knew the best thrust
into our spread open souls
and, gasping, found themselves floundering, those
men
and their knowing.
they forgot how to float on our intimate oceans, on
the tides
marked by blood
and birth, by the keening and the crescent silver-lit
sky.
they feared
our boundlessness, our eons of always, the
foreverness
of now.
they looked into our eyes and saw stardust and
strength
and have been
trembling ever since. in that squalor of fear they
spun
lies and we

believed, and shrank. but now the false unfurls
and we remember
our cosmic lineage. we lift our voices into the
silence, shattering,

and howl.

THE LIGHT

(or something like it)

on rising

the phoenix is just a bird
until she cracks from the fire,
feathers sticky with soul-
blood and promise and all that rising --

stretching a still-soft new
talon, it steps from what was to
what could be, weeping
when the raging embers
of promise meet vulnerable flesh --

a step, and another, she keeps
moving toward uncertain, fleshy
hope until her wings spread dry
enough for flying, knowing that rebirth
always hurts, is worth enduring, is
made ever possible solely by the burning --

incarnation

i am made to bleed, you see,
to ache and sweat and sing. sinews
stretch sacred in the dawning,
spirit and skin becoming
one.

can you feel it? you are
clammy-palmed holy. insecurity
is an anointing. you don't have
to be perfect to be good, to be
loved.

fifty shades of doubt and we are
hauling soul over grit and glass
on shredding knees. but
we know we are coming home
at last.

reflections from a shop of recycled homewares

sacred space, hallowed refuse stacked
holy and reaching, refusing to limp languid
into obscurity, fearless of the flaccidity
of age. derelict doors slouch
one on another on another, piled
panes and panels, painted knobs,
sinks and splintered wood lumbered along
their shelves, stained and grout-marked, and

acceptance is a slow death, they know.
they won't enliven the lie that their faded
beauty equates ugly, unwanted, out-ripened life
to be forfeited with all docility. wrinkled

and worn deep with the gritted glory
of moments tumbled soul-thick across
time and skin, Dignity, Value, and Wisdom
are the only songs this abandoned
vintage breathe into glorious color.

The Gray Hair

I glance into the glass,
an offhand toss of a thing,
and she introduces herself,
soft as a whisper, undeniable
as the moon. Silver,

she twines through the dark
chestnut solidarity of her sisters
and does not fear to stand
alone, to gleam apart, wholly
herself. My breath catches

a moment, tangled in the web
of all I've been taught to think
of unyouth. Then – the moment
slides by like a sigh, and I smile
and welcome her home.

playing house

for a night we pretend,
play at three becoming we again,
as if my body had never been
the soil to your seeds,
expanding like a universe,
dark and wet and breaking
open in screams of hope
and terror, as if
I could forget my heart
birthed flesh and baby bone,
as if my chest is not
a fearsome cavern of claws
and maternal proclivities.

but we pack him off for a half-turn
of the moon and sun anyway. I run
crimson over these lips and you
wind your arm about my waist
when I lean against you, lovers
for an evening. I close
my eyes and remember how it was
before the thickening
of my womb. I anticipate

freedom, spirit salivating.

instead that other path we didn't
walk yawns too wide without
all the life
in those sleepless nights, without
the way he clambers up
my back for a horsey ride
sometimes, without
velvet cheeks and eyes like the sky
and tendrils scented sour-sweet
tucked beneath my chin as we read
together. I shudder
at the ossification of the soul
absent all that wonder

his being birthed in me,
in we, and, in hungry gratitude,
make my heart a bed for his
all over again.

red

sometimes
there is an ache
between my legs
(you know where)
reminiscent of crowning
joy and agony, the first
breath (or not), and I
miss that moment
between
here and
There,
where sacred and salt kissed
my screaming skin as one,
and I knew even then
that I was birthing more than the exquisite
miracle of that slate-eyed boy, but
also my
self.
or
maybe that was
conception
and I have been gestating,
laboring wild in all

the searing, sweeping, glory-
bathed months since.

my boy, he is
tall and heavy, walking, why
he has practically grown all the way
up and
so have I.

my cervix opened
a door to my heart and forever
and we walked
in (out) together.
I am who I am, finally
(almost)
back arched and aching over
unending mundanity,
mining miracles.

I am the wild Mother.

I am

I am the long dark night
I am the soul in peril
I am the corrupted collective conscience
I am the Rubicon, the highest water
I am the rebel general
I am the suicidal stand
I am the lovelorn witness, the wailing
daughters of wisdom and wild
I am the shorn first
I am the staccato tattoo, the ebony ink
I am the limp unfurling
I am the flaccid spirit of unrest
I am the bear and the giant and the worm
I am the desolate and the desolation
I am the rejected hope, the silenced
scream, the fleeting peace, the unceasing
battle
I am the you and the me and the we
I am the deep way, the blackened path, the only
road
up.

I am the here, blooming beneath

your trembling fingers if only
you'd trail them along this
skin. I could be your ecstasy, our
crimson heat, my own undoing,
if you'd turn this way.

a blessing for the living

may you know that courage
is a choice, that fearlessness is
not the stage of breathing-being fear-
less but tasting the metallic tang
of panic on the tongue and
breathing dancing stretching
leaping limping walking
painting panting giving
telling loving love-making
hoping healing asking
flying falling forgetting
forgiving recalling knowing
craving crying hungering
laughing howling hurting
changing choosing
resting
rising
growing going
eating entering learning
breaking being
wanting waning hunting
claiming clamoring embracing
emanating lighting

up this graying world with all
your glorious, gleaming you-ness
anyway.

cadence

when I feel old
I return
I return
I return
to the air
sweeping in
and through
my body

I return
to the waters
crimson and deep
running in
and through
my body

I return
to the light, to
the sun-soaked breath
washing into
and through
my body

I return
to the earth
to the rich
fertile mire
pulsing into
and through
my body

and find
in the end
that life again
begins, rushing into
and through
my body

the god I'll bow down to

I hear a whisper
in the walls.
is it my wishing
or is Someone
there, creeping
in close from the cosmos?
all my prayers are
a moldy fantasy,
and I've stopped
listening for replies
as clear as the sky
in winter, spreading itself thick
and aloof above
the snow. but,
gasping fears of my
own grave aside,
I don't mind. when
I can choose
courage, the murk
of mystery is always
the god I'll bow down to, pressing
this forehead to
the earth, giddy

with not-knowing.

song for the darkness

look for the light. honor the darkness. you were
born for this. you were born for the wild things.
color and rhythm coalesce. you change the world
by breathing.

believe you. believe this.

do not be afraid. even to the thickest dark dawn
comes now and again, clear and bright, a
cacophony of seeing. the birds are awake. their
song begins. you are not alone.

breathe true. bleed true.
remember your body, its skin spreading over your
soul, your pulse power. you are good medicine.

move your limbs languid, dance the brush through
paint and across paper, unfurl your words.
listen, really listen, to the deep knowing that speaks
from the belly. it is no accident that life begins here.

trust your soul's fertility. no matter what the body
can or cannot birth, you are never fallow.

let your heart-womb shed and thicken and then,
groaning joy, bring forth all your hopes, all that
your bones know is yours to bring into being.

you are mother, you are father. you light this world
on fire.

awaken.
revel in the heat of your own flames. feel the drum
beat throbbing in your gut, the searing nearness of
the sacred fires, the slap of your bared soles against
earth as you dance in the ash and embers of your
own waking.

you were made for the light, for spirit and sinew,
for the uncertain dark, for hands holding hands
holding hands.

the song begins. you are not alone.

ACKNOWLEDGEMENTS

Thank you to Jamie Bonilla, Heather Mattern, and Erin Housewright for being my beta readers. You are amazing.

Thanks also to The Inkwell and The Coterie online writing communities, for reminding me that I could do it.

And thank you to my readers of my blog and previous books, to the fans of my artwork and related projects, and those who follow along on social media. Thank you for listening, for asking for more, for cheering me on, and for your care. I don't think I could have come this far without you.

COPYRIGHT ACKNOLWEDGEMENTS

"the wildest one" was previously published in The Phoenix Soul Online Magazine, 2014.

"wrestling rusted doubt" was previously published on www.bethmorey.com, 2013, and in *To Linger On Hot Coals*, 2013.

"in between: was previously published on in *To Linger On Hot Coals*, 2013.

"rainbow" was previously published in *To Linger On Hot Coals*, 2013.

"Pathways to God" was previously published on The Secret Rebel Club blog (now defunct).

"my words are a whisper, my words are a howl" was previously published on The Secret Rebel Club blog (now defunct).

"lives" was previously published in The Phoenix

Soul Online Magazine, 2014.

"rustlings" was previously published in The
Phoenix Soul Online Magazine, 2015.

"spoiled epiphanies (or, when the poet is broken)"
was previously published in *To Linger On Hot Coals*,
2013.

"lineage" was previously published in The Phoenix
Soul Online Magazine, 2014.

"on the impossible" was previously published in
The Phoenix Soul Online Magazine, 2015.

"egress" was previously published in The Phoenix
Soul Online Magazine, 2014.

"on rising" was previously published in The
Phoenix Soul Online Magazine, 2015.

"incarnation" was previously published on The
Secret Rebel Club blog (now defunct).

"cadence" was previously published in The Phoenix

Soul Online Magazine, 2015.

Many, many thanks to the editors of the above publications, for believing in my words, giving them a home, and encouraging me to keep going.

51746681R00062

Made in the USA
San Bernardino, CA
31 July 2017